THINGS PIANO PLAYERS Really WANT TO Say But Can't

Copyright © 2022
All rights reserved. No part of this publication may be reproduced, distributed, or transmitted in any form or by any means, including photocopying, recording, or other electronic or mechanical methods, without the prior or written permission of the publisher

WAKE UP AND BE A Fucking AWESOME

Be Strong
BELIEVE in YOURSELF

Be the Light

You're amazing

Smile More. Worry Fucking Less!

WAKE UP AND BE A FUCKING AWESOME PIANO PLAYER

opportunities Are All AROUND ME

Spread Love EVERYWHERE YOU FUCKING Go

YOU ARE Awesome As FUCK

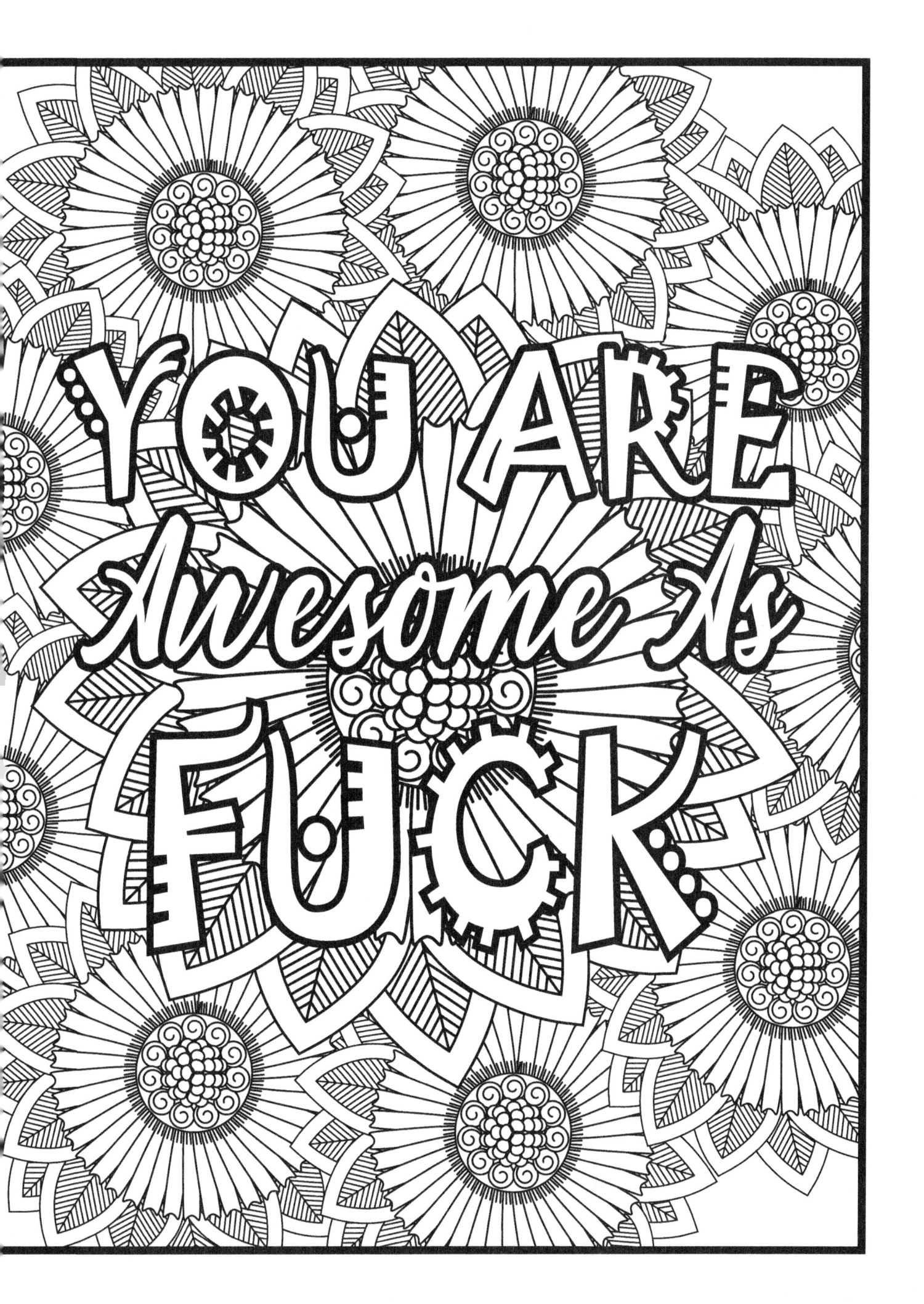

Let That Shit go

You Are A Fucking Rock

be happy IT DRIVES ASSHOLES crazy

Cheer The Fuck Up

TAKE NO SHITS. GIVE NO FUCKS.

I Gave Zero Fucks Today

SLAY ALL MOTHER FUCKING DAY

CALM THE Fuck Down & Color

Hey Fuckface Do Some Work

Dealing with your **BULLSHIT** isn't in my job Description

The Best is yet to FUCKING COME

I'm A Kind OF A FUCKING GREAT Deal

Fuck Off

Test Your Colors

☆ ☆ ☆ ☆ ☆
Don't forget to
give us your opinion
By leaving a review

Printed in Great Britain
by Amazon